Sweet Mania®

by
Cathy Prange
and
Joan Pauli

Published and Distributed by
Muffin Mania Publishing Co.,
553 Greenbrook Dr.,
Kitchener, Ontario. N2M 4K5

Printed by Ainsworth Press,
Kitchener, Ontario

Cover Photograph by Jan Pisarczyk,
Pirak Studios

Art Direction, Food Styling and
Illustrations by Judith Elsasser

I.S.B.N.   0-9691485-5-0

Cover Photograph

Sweet Mania

When you know "they" are coming, BRING ON DESSERT!

How do you end a meal? It's sweet, rich, luscious and brings a twinkle to the eye. . . it's Sweet Mania!

Even though we are all diet conscious, we still crave a sweet treat and like to indulge without a twinge of guilt.

We have again compiled only our very favourite, easy to make recipes, including our Christmas goodies, baked and shared with each other for years. We now invite you to share them with us.

How Sweet It Is:

To have so many fans who have asked, "What's next?"

To have as many guys as gals demanding equal recognition in the kitchen and rightfully so!

To be remembered for our old fashioned, homey, easy to prepare recipes.

To be even better Sisters, Partners and Friends!

Cathy Prange
Joan Pauli

Table Of Contents

Table of contents (continued):

Table of contents (continued):

Table of contents (continued):

Cookies and Bars

Table of contents (continued):

Christmas Goodies

Pies

Apple Pizza Pie

5 apples, peeled, cored and sliced
1/2 c. white sugar
1 tsp. cinnamon

3/4 c. flour
1/2 c. white sugar
6 1/2 tbsp. butter or margarine
1 c. cheddar cheese, shredded

Line a pizza pan with pastry.

In a small bowl, mix the sugar and cinnamon lightly with the apples and fill pastry-lined pan.

Mix the flour, white sugar and butter or margarine until crumbly and sprinkle on top of apple mixture.

Bake at 400° for 15 minutes. Decrease heat to 375° and continue baking for 30 minutes.

Top with 1 cup of cheddar cheese and heat until the cheese melts.

Serve warm.

Serve in wedges like pizza.
Kids love it!

Mom's Dutch Apple Pie

1 unbaked pie shell
4 - 5 good cooking apples
cinnamon
1/2 c. white sugar
1/2 c. brown sugar
2 tbsp. flour
carnation milk
sour cream

Peel, core and quarter apples.

Line pie shell with apples, filling the spaces with smaller pieces of apple.

Sprinkle with cinnamon.

In a small bowl, mix together white sugar, brown sugar and flour. Add enough carnation milk until pouring consistency and add a dollop of sour cream. Mix well and pour over apples.

Dot with butter and sprinkle with brown sugar.

Bake at 350° for 45 minutes or until brown and apples are cooked.

Mom served this with a piece of old cheddar.
Dad said, "Apple Pie without cheese is like a kiss without a squeeze!"

Mother Barker's Unbaked Apple Pie

1 baked 9" pie shell
1 1/2 c. apple juice
3/4 c. white sugar
2 tbsp. corn starch
1 tbsp. butter
1/2 tsp. vanilla
7 - 10 medium apples
1 c. whipping cream
1/2 tsp. cinnamon or nutmeg

Peel apples and cut into eighths.

In saucepan, bring 1 1/4 c. apple juice to a boil. Reduce heat and add one-half of the apple wedges.

Bring to a boil and cook until apples are tender and firm, but not soft (about 5 minutes).

Remove apples with a slotted spoon and drain. Repeat with the remaining apples.

Stir together corn starch and remaining 1/4 c. apple juice and stir into juice in the saucepan. Bring to a boil and stir until thickened, stirring constantly.

Add butter and vanilla and allow to cool.

Arrange 1/2 of the apple wedges over bottom of baked pie shell and drizzle over one-half of the glaze.

Repeat with remaining apples and glaze and chill until set.

When ready to serve, whip cream, adding cinnamon or nutmeg and spread on pie.

Unbaked Blueberry Pie

1 9" baked pastry shell
1 quart blueberries
1 c. white sugar
3 tbsp. corn starch
1/4 tsp. salt
1/4 c. water
1 tsp. lemon juice
1 tbsp. butter

Put 2 c. raw blueberries into baked pastry shell.

Mix sugar, corn starch, salt and water together and add remaining 2 c. blueberries.

Cook until thickened.

Remove from heat and add lemon juice and butter.

Pour cooked blueberries over the raw blueberries in shell.

Serve with whipped cream.

Variation: Make a graham wafer crust,
pack into a 9" square baking pan and cut in squares.
This is wonderful! Use either fresh or frozen blueberries.

Irish Coffee Pie

1 3 1/2 oz. package of vanilla instant pudding
2 tsp. instant coffee powder
1/2 c. cold milk
1/3 c. water
3 tbsp. Irish Whisky, rum or brandy
1/2 c. whipping cream
1 8" baked pastry shell

In a bowl combine pudding mix and coffee powder.

Add milk and beat at high speed for 1 minute.

Blend in the water and whisky and beat at high speed for 2 minutes more or until fluffy.

Whip cream and fold into prepared filling.

Pile into pie shell and chill 3 to 4 hours.

Garnish with whipped cream and chocolate shavings.

Cheers!
Better than a cup of Irish Coffee!
Don't wait until St. Patrick's Day to serve this one!

Ann's Lemon Sponge Pie

1 unbaked pie shell
1 c. white sugar
2 tsp. flour
3 tbsp. butter, melted
2 egg yolks
1 lemon — rind and juice
1 c. milk
2 egg whites, beaten

Mix sugar, flour, butter and egg yolks.

Add lemon (juice and rind) and milk and mix again.

Fold in the beaten egg whites.

Pour into unbaked pie shell and bake at 375° for 30-45 minutes or until set.

A very economical pie.
Our friend Ann Baird served us this pie often
in the "good old days!"

Key Lime Pie

1 9" baked pastry shell
1 can condensed milk
4 eggs, separated
   — keeping one egg white in a separate container
1/2 c. lime juice

Mix together condensed milk, 4 egg yolks and lime juice.

Beat 1 egg white stiff and fold into the above.

Pour into baked pastry shell.

Beat remaining 3 egg whites until stiff, gradually adding 6 tbsp. sugar and 1/2 tsp. cream of tartar.

Pile on top of filling and bake at 350° until meringue is golden brown, approximately 5 minutes.

Pictured on our cover,
this is an original Florida Keys outstanding dessert.

Nesselrode Pie

1 9" baked pastry shell
1 envelope unflavoured gelatin
2/3 c. white sugar, divided
1/8 tsp. salt
3 eggs, separated
1 1/4 c. milk
1 c. cream (half and half)
2 tsp. rum flavouring, or 3 tbsp. rum or sherry
3 tbsp. chopped maraschino cherries or chopped glazed fruit
2 tbsp. shaved chocolate

Mix gelatin, 1/3 c. sugar and salt thoroughly in top of double boiler.

Beat egg yolks, milk and the cream together and add to the gelatin mixture.

Cook over boiling water, stirring constantly until gelatin is dissolved, about 5 minutes. Remove from heat and stir in desired flavouring.

Chill in refrigerator, stirring occasionally until mixture mounds when dropped from a spoon. (about 1 hour).

Beat egg whites until stiff. Beat in remaining 1/3 c. sugar.

Fold gelatin mixture and 1 1/2 tbsp. of the cherries into stiffly beaten egg whites and turn into baked pie shell.

Spinkle remaining cherries over the surface and press in lightly with the back of a spoon.

Top with whipped cream and sprinkle with shaved chocolate.

Anna's Peach Pie

1 unbaked pie shell
1/2 c. brown sugar
1 c. flour
1/4 c. butter
4 - 5 c. sliced peaches

Cut the butter into flour and brown sugar until mixture is crumbly.

Place 1/2 of the crumb mixture into pie shell.

Place sliced peaches on top.

Cream together: 1 c. sour cream and
                  1 c. brown sugar

Pour over peaches and sprinkle with remaining half of the crumb mixture.

Bake at 425° for 10 minutes.

Lower heat to 350° and bake for 30 minutes.

Mother's friend Anna, served this for their Dessert Bridge Club, and shared this old fashioned recipe with us.

Fresh Peach Pie

1 unbaked pie shell
4 - 5 c. sliced peaches
1/2 c. white sugar
3 tbsp. flour
1 c. sour cream

Fill pie shell with sliced peaches.

Mix together sugar, flour and sour cream and pour over peaches.

Bake at 425° for 15 minutes.

Lower heat to 350° and bake for 30 minutes or until set.

Sprinkle 1/4 c. brown sugar on top and place under broiler until brown.

Watch closely as the sugar burns quickly!

M–m–m–good! What a peach of a pie!

Pecan Pie

1 unbaked pie shell
3 eggs
2/3 c. brown sugar
1/2 tsp. salt
1/3 c. melted butter
1 c. corn syrup
1 tsp. vanilla or rum
1 1/2 c. pecan halves

Spread pecans over the pastry shell.

Combine eggs, sugar, salt, butter and corn syrup. Add vanilla or rum and beat well.

Pour over pecans.

Bake at 425° for 10 minutes.

Lower heat to 350° and continue baking for 30 minutes or until set.

Cool. Serve with whipped cream or ice cream.

Irresistible! Be sure to save room for a slice of this prize winning Southern pecan pie!

Auntie Lib's Pumpkin Pie

1 unbaked pastry shell
1 1/2 c. pumpkin (14 oz. can)
3 eggs
1/2 c. white sugar
1/2 c. brown sugar
1/4 tsp. salt
1/2 tsp. cinnamon
1/4 tsp. ginger
1/4 tsp. nutmeg
1/4 tsp. ground cloves
1 small can carnation milk (160 ml)

Beat eggs and add sugar, spices and salt. Mix well.

Stir in pumpkin and carnation milk. Beat well.

Pour into pastry shell and bake at 400° for 30 minutes.

Reduce heat to 350° and continue baking for 25 minutes or until filling is set.

This brings back fond memories of our childhood; Sunday dinners at the old farm near Linwood.

Margie's Sour Cream Raisin Pie

1 unbaked 8" pie shell
1 c. white sugar
1 egg
1/2 tsp. vanilla
1 c. sour cream
1 c. raisins
pinch salt

Beat sugar and egg together and add vanilla.

Add raisins, sour cream and salt and blend together.

Pour into unbaked pie shell.

Bake at 400° for 10 minutes.

Reduce heat to 350° and bake until knife inserted in the centre comes out clean and custard is set — about 20 minutes.

Top with whipped cream.

Everyone loves raisin pie!
A nice change from the traditional raisin pie!

Rhubarb Custard Pie

1 9" unbaked pastry shell
4 c. rhubarb (cut in 1" slices)
1 1/2 c. white sugar
1/4 c. flour
dash nutmeg and salt
3 eggs, beaten
2 tbsp. butter

Mix together sugar, flour, nutmeg and salt.

Add 3 beaten eggs and beat until smooth.

Stir in 4 cups rhubarb.

Fill pastry shell with rhubarb mixture and dot with 2 tbsp. butter.

Bake at 400° for 10 minutes.

Reduce heat to 350° and bake for 40 minutes or until custard is set.

There is nothing like the first fresh rhubarb pie!
Our kids seem to know when the rhubarb patch is ready!
They drive miles for a slice of this pie!

Auntie Thelma's Strawberry Pie

1 9" baked pie shell
1 quart of strawberries
1 c. sugar
2 tbsp. corn starch
1 tbsp. butter
1/2 tsp. salt

Arrange 1/2 quart of raw berries in the pie shell.

In a saucepan mix sugar, corn starch, butter and salt.

Mash remaining strawberries and add to mixture in the saucepan.

Cook until thickened and pour over berries in the pie shell.

Serve with whipped cream.

Another fond childhood memory.
Whenever we serve this pie, we remember good times and
good food, at Auntie Thelma's in Mitchell.

Cakes

Apple Chunk Cake

1/2 c. butter or margarine
1 1/2 c. white sugar
2 eggs well beaten
1 1/2 c. flour
1 tsp. cinnamon
1 tsp. nutmeg
1/2 tsp. salt
2 tsp. baking soda
1 c. 100% All Bran cereal
4 c. chopped apples

Cream margarine and sugar. Add eggs and beat until creamy. Add flour, spices, salt and soda.

Mix in the bran along with the chopped apples.

Pour batter into greased 9" × 13" pan and bake at 350° for 40 minutes.

Sauce
1/2 c. butter
1 c. white sugar
2 beaten eggs
3/4 c. sherry
1 tsp. lemon rind
pinch of nutmeg

Melt butter and add sugar and beaten eggs. Beat well.

Stir in sherry and lemon rind. Cook slowly, stirring until thickened.

Serve cake with a scoop of ice cream and pour hot sauce over the ice cream.

Lebanese Applesauce Cake

1 lb. seedless raisins
2 c. applesauce
2 tsp. baking soda
1/2 tsp. salt
2 tsp. cinnamon
2 tsp. nutmeg
2 tsp. allspice
3 1/2 c. flour
2 c. sugar
1 c. pecans
4 tbsp. butter, melted

Preheat oven to 350°

Cover raisins with water and cook until water is gone. Set aside and cool.

Put the applesauce in a bowl and stir in baking soda. It will double, turn foamy and darken.

Mix salt, cinnamon, nutmeg, allspice and flour.

Add sugar to applesauce, then add the flour mixture slowly and combine well.

Add raisins, pecans and melted butter.

Pour batter in greased tube pan and bake at 350° for two hours.

Makes a 5 lb. cake.

Best when aged in tin for one week.

Grandma Milner's Banana Cake

1/2 c. butter or margarine
1 c. white sugar
2 well beaten eggs
1 c. mashed bananas (3 medium)
1/2 c. sour milk
1 tsp. baking soda (dissolved in the sour milk)
2 c. flour
2 tsp. baking powder
1/4 tsp. salt
1 tsp. vanilla

Cream butter or margarine and sugar.

Add beaten eggs and mashed bananas.

Mix flour, baking powder and salt together and add to the creamed mixture alternately with the mixture of sour milk and baking soda.

Always start and end with the flour.

Add vanilla.

Pour batter into a 9" greased and floured square pan and bake at 350° for 30-40 minutes.

Ice when cool with a butter icing.

Grandma Milner always added a couple of tablespoons of peanut butter to her butter icing. Like her banana muffins, this is truly our family's favourite!

Carrot Cake

4 medium-size carrots
1/2 c. chopped nuts (we prefer pecans)
2 c. flour
1 1/2 tsp. baking soda
2 tsp. baking powder
2 tsp. cinnamon
1 tsp. salt
2 c. white sugar
4 eggs
1 1/2 c. salad oil
1 small can crushed pineapple, drained

Preheat oven to 350°.

Grease and flour a 10" bundt pan or a 9" × 13" baking pan.

Peel and grate carrots. You should have about two cups.

Add nuts to carrots and set aside.

Measure dry ingredients (flour, baking soda, baking powder, cinnamon and salt) into a large bowl. Mix well with a fork.

Beat sugar and eggs. Add oil and beat well.

Pour oil mixture over dry ingredients and mix well with spoon.

Stir in shredded carrots, nuts and drained pineapple.

Pour batter into pan and bake at 350° for 45-50 minutes or until wooden pick comes out clean.

Cool 15 minutes before removing from pan.

Ice with cream cheese frosting, if desired.

continued. . .

Carrot Cake (continued)

Cream Cheese Frosting
1 small package cream cheese, softened
1/4 c. softened butter
2 c. icing sugar
1 tbsp. marmalade

Cream together cream cheese and butter.

Blend in icing sugar and beat well.

Stir in marmalade.

The whole world loves carrot cake!
This is without a doubt our favourite carrot cake recipe,
with or without the icing! Serve a "hunk" to-day!

May's Chocolate Zucchini Cake

4 oz. unsweetened chocolate
1 1/2 c. salad oil
3 c. white sugar
4 eggs
3 c. grated zucchini
3 c. flour
1 1/2 tsp. baking powder
1 tsp. baking soda
1 tsp. salt
1 c. finely chopped pecans

Melt chocolate over hot water.

Mix oil and sugar together and add eggs. Beat for 2 minutes.

Beat in zucchini.

Mix dry ingredients together and add to zucchini mixture.

Add the melted chocolate and nuts.

Pour batter into greased bundt pan and bake at 350° for
1 hour and 15 minutes or until wooden pick comes out clean.

Remove from oven and let cool for 15 minutes before removing
from pan.

Moist and delicious like Carrot Cake, and freezes well!

Donna's German Chocolate Cake

1 1/4 c. boiling water
1 c. oatmeal
1/2 c. margarine
6 oz. chocolate chips

Mix the above ingredients in a bowl and let stand for 20 minutes.

1 1/2 c. flour
1 c. white sugar
1 tsp. baking soda
1/2 tsp. salt
3 eggs, beaten

Mix the flour, sugar, baking soda and salt.

Add beaten eggs and oatmeal mixture and beat well.

Pour into a greased 9" × 13" pan and bake at 350° for 35 minutes, until top is firm.

Icing
6 tbsp. butter or margarine
1/4 c. cream
3/4 c. brown sugar
1/2 c. chopped pecans

Mix the butter, cream and sugar in a saucepan and cook for 3 minutes, until slightly thickened. Add the nuts.

Pour over cake and broil until bubbly about 3 minutes. Watch carefully. Cool.

Hot Fudge Sundae Cake

1 c. all purpose flour
2 tsp. baking powder
1/4 tsp. salt
3/4 c. sugar
2 tbsp. cocoa
1/2 c. milk
2 tbsp. salad oil
1/2 tsp. vanilla
1 c. chopped nuts
1/2 c. chocolate chips
1 c. brown sugar
1/4 c. cocoa
1 3/4 c. boiling water

Preheat oven to 350°.

Mix the flour, baking powder, salt, sugar and 2 tbsp. cocoa in a bowl.

Stir in milk, oil, vanilla, nuts and chocolate chips and spread in a 9" square baking pan.

Combine the brown sugar and 1/4 c. cocoa and sprinkle over batter.

Carefully pour boiling water over all and bake 40 minutes or until cake springs back when touched.

Serve warm or cold with whipped cream.

Delicious! Makes its own sauce!
This recipe was sent to us by our friend, Barb Logsdail, who is a freelance writer in Saskatoon and a noted cook book author.

Irish Coffee Cake

1/2 c. margarine
1 c. white sugar
2 eggs
2 c. flour
1 tsp. baking soda
1 tsp. baking powder
1/2 tsp. salt
1 tsp. vanilla
1 c. sour cream

Topping
1/3 c. brown sugar
1/4 c. white sugar
1 tsp. cinnamon
1 c. chopped nuts

Cream margarine and sugar. Add eggs and beat well.

Add the sifted dry ingredients alternately with sour cream. Always start and end with the flour. Add vanilla.

Pour one-half of the batter into a well greased tube or bundt pan. Cover with one-half the topping.

Spread remaining batter over and the rest of the topping.

Bake 350° for 40 minutes.

Another recipe from the "good old days".
We often add sliced apples to the batter —m—m—m—good!

Joye's Dump Cake

1 - 19 oz. can crushed pineapple, undrained
1 - 19 oz. can cherry, apple or raspberry pie filling
1 - 19 oz. pouch yellow cake mix
1/2 c. slivered almonds
1/2 c. butter

Pour the crushed pineapple into a 9" × 12" cake pan, spreading evenly.

Pour pie filling evenly over pineapple.

Sprinkle cake mix over the pie filling.

Sprinkle slivered almonds over cake.

Cut butter into chunks and dot on top.

Bake at 350° for 1 hour, or until done.

We like to keep these ingredients on hand.
Quick and easy if friends or family drop in unexpectedly.
No need to be without a delicious dessert!
Just dump, dump, dump!

Carol's Oatmeal Spice Cake

1 c. oatmeal
1 c. boiling water
1/2 c. butter or margarine
2 c. brown sugar
2 eggs
1 c. flour
1 tsp. baking soda
1/2 tsp. salt
1/2 tsp. cinnamon
1/4 tsp. nutmeg
1/4 tsp. cloves
1/2 c. raisins
1/2 c. walnuts

Pour boiling water over the oatmeal and let stand for 30 minutes.

Cream butter and brown sugar. Add the eggs and beat well.

Mix the dry ingredients together with the spices and add to the creamed mixture alternately with the oatmeal mixture.

Fold in raisins and nuts.

Pour batter into 9" × 13" greased pan and bake at 350° for 40-50 minutes.

Brown Sugar Icing
Melt 1 tbsp. butter, 1 tbsp. cream and 3/4 c. brown sugar.

Add icing sugar to spread and 1 tsp. vanilla.

Ice cake and sprinkle with coconut.

(Or use same icing as on German Chocolate Cake).

Princess of Wales Cake

1 c. dates or raisins
1 c. boiling water
1/4 c. butter or margarine
1 c. white sugar
1 egg
1 1/2 c. flour
1 tsp. baking powder
3/4 tsp. baking soda
pinch of salt
1/2 c. nuts

Pour boiling water over dates and let stand until cool.

Cream butter and sugar. Beat in egg.

Stir together dry ingredients and add to the creamed mixture alternately with date mixture.

Fold in nuts.

Pour batter in greased and floured 9" square pan. Bake 350° for 40-50 minutes.

Topping
3 tbsp. brown sugar
3 tbsp. butter
2 tbsp. cream
1/2 c. coconut

Mix together and spread on warm cake. Put cake back in oven and place under broiler until brown. Watch carefully for fear of burning.

Definitely a Royal Cake — sturdy and substantial.
We wonder if Di has ever made this!

Rhubarb Cake

2 1/2 c. rhubarb, cut in 1" pieces
2 c. flour
1 1/4 c. white sugar
1 tsp. baking soda
1/2 tsp. salt
2 eggs
1 c. sour cream

Topping
1 c. brown sugar
1/4 c. flour
1/4 c. softened butter
cinnamon

Mix together the dry ingredients.

In another bowl, mix eggs and sour cream.

Add the dry ingredients to the wet and then add the rhubarb. The batter will be heavy.

Pour into a greased and floured 9" × 13" pan and sprinkle with the topping.

Sprinkle with cinnamon.

Bake at 350° for 45 minutes.

RAH! RAH! RHUBARB
What a way to get your Spring Tonic!

Thel's Sponge Cake

2 eggs, separated
4 tbsp. cold water
1 c. white sugar
1 c. flour
1 tsp. baking powder
1 tsp. vanilla

Beat egg yolks and add 4 tbsp. cold water and 1 c. white sugar.

Mix flour and baking powder and add to above.

Beat egg whites until stiff and add vanilla.

Fold into batter.

Pour batter into ungreased 9" square pan and bake at 350° for 30 minutes.

*A super summertime sponge cake.
We serve it like a shortcake with fresh fruit and whipped cream.*

Tomato Soup Cake

3/4 c. butter or margarine
1 1/2 c. white sugar
1 can tomato soup
3/4 c. water
3 c. flour
1 tsp. baking soda
3 tsp. baking powder
pinch salt
1 1/2 tsp. cinnamon
1 1/2 tsp. nutmeg
1 tsp. cloves
1 1/2 c. raisins
1 1/2 c. chopped nuts
1 c. maraschino cherries cut in half

Cream butter and sugar.

Mix tomato soup and water together.

Stir together flour and rest of dry ingredients.

Add dry ingredients to creamed mixture alternately with soup and water mixture.

Add raisins, nuts and cherries.

Pour into greased bundt pan and bake 350° for one hour.

Cool well before removing from pan.

This recipe was sent to us from our friend Margie and of all the versions of this cake, we liked hers the best. Will keep indefinitely in a cool place.

Wacky Cake

1 1/2 c. flour
1 c. white sugar
3 tbsp. cocoa
1 tsp. baking powder
1 tsp. baking soda
1/4 tsp. salt

Sift all above ingredients into an ungreased 9" square pan.

Make three holes with a spoon.

Into one, put 1 tbsp. vinegar, into the second, 5 tbsp. melted butter and into the third, 1 tsp. vanilla.

Pour 1 c. lukewarm water over all and stir until blended.

Bake 350° for one-half hour.

<u>Icing</u>
3/4 c. white sugar
pinch of salt
2 tbsp. cornstarch
1 tbsp. cocoa

Mix all ingredients in a saucepan and add 1 c. hot water. Cook until thick and add 1 tbsp. butter and 1 tsp. vanilla.

Spread on cake while still warm.

No fuss, no muss! A favourite with kids of all ages!

Special
Desserts

Almond Crunch

1/2 c. butter
2 c. Cap'n Crunch cereal
1 c. coconut
1 c. slivered almonds
3/4 c. brown sugar

1/2 gal. vanilla ice cream, softened

Place first five ingredients in frying pan and stir at medium heat until golden brown.

While warm, press one-half of mixture into a 9" × 13" pan.

Spread ice cream over and top with remaining crumb mixture.

Cut in serving size squares.

Freeze.

Ice cream desserts are ideal when refrigerators are jammed with holiday goodies at home or cottage. So look to your freezer to hold make-ahead desserts. They are a cool and refreshing ending to a hot meal!

Anna's Dessert

1 1/4 c. graham wafer crumbs
1/4 c. brown sugar
1/3 c. softened or melted butter

Mix together and press into a 9" square pan, reserving 1/4 c. crumbs for the top.

Bake at 350° for 5 minutes.

Filling
1 small pkg. cream cheese moistened with 2 tbsp. milk
1 small pkg. vanilla instant pudding mix
1 pkg. dream whip
2 c. cold milk
1/2 tsp. vanilla

Beat above ingredients together until thick and add 1/2 tsp. vanilla.

Pour one-half of the above mixture onto the cooled crumbs.

Pour 1 can cherry pie filling over the creamed mixture.

Top with remaining cream cheese mixture and then remaining crumbs.

Chill.

Should be made the day before you wish to serve. Delicious!

Old-Fashioned Apple Dumplings

6 medium-sized baking apples
2 c. flour
2 1/2 tsp. baking powder
1/2 tsp. salt
2/3 c. shortening
1/2 c. milk

Pare and core apples.

Pastry
Stir flour, baking powder and salt together.

Cut in shortening with pastry blender or two knives until crumbly.

Sprinkle milk over mixture and press dough together just until it holds.

Roll out dough and cut into 6 squares.

Place an apple on each square.

Fill cavity in apple with sugar and cinnamon.

Pat dough around apple to cover completely and fasten edges.

Place dumplings 1" apart in greased baking dish and pour sauce over. Bake 375° for 40 minutes, basting occasionally with the sauce.

Serve hot.

Sauce: 2 c. brown sugar
         2 c. water
         1/4 c. butter
         1/4 tsp. cinnamon or nutmeg

Combine brown sugar, water and cinnamon in saucepan and cook for 5 minutes. Remove from heat and add butter.

Banana Split Dessert

Meringue
3 egg whites
3/4 c. white sugar
1/2 tsp. vanilla
1/4 tsp. vinegar

Filling
1 c. mashed ripe bananas
1/4 tsp. salt
2 tbsp. lemon juice
1 c. whipping cream whipped with 1/4 c. icing sugar

Preheat oven to 275°.

Beat egg whites until stiff and gradually beat in the sugar.

Add vanilla and vinegar and beat well.

Cut two 8" circles out of waxed paper and place on baking sheet.

Divide egg whites equally between them, spreading meringue to almost cover paper rounds.

Bake at 275° for 45-50 minutes or until golden brown.

Allow to cool. Place meringue on a damp towel, wait a few minutes and remove from waxed paper.

Allow to cool completely.

continued. . .

Banana Split Dessert (continued)

Banana Filling
Combine the filling ingredients in a small bowl.

Place one meringue on serving plate and cover with filling.

Top with second meringue.

Wrap in foil and freeze at least three hours or until filling is set like ice cream.

To Serve
Remove from freezer 25 minutes ahead of time and garnish with sliced strawberries or raspberries and hot chocolate sauce.

Chocolate Sauce
4 squares semi-sweet chocolate
2 tbsp. butter
1/4 c. corn syrup
1/3 c. coffee liquer
1/4 c. whipping cream

Combine all ingredients in saucepan and simmer gently for 20 minutes.

This keeps in refrigerator and can be reheated.

OR

Drizzle with chocolate sauce of your choice.

Black Forest Squares

1 pkg. chocolate cake mix (one layer size)
1 carton sour cream (8 oz. size)
1 pkg. (4 serving size) instant chocolate pudding
1 c. milk
1/4 c. tia maria
1 can cherry pie filling (19 oz. size)
1/2 c. whipping cream
1/4 c. toasted, slivered almonds

Mix cake mix according to directions on the package.

Bake in greased 9" × 13" pan at 350° for 15-20 minutes.

Beat sour cream, chocolate pudding, 1/3 c. of the milk and tia maria until fluffy.

Add remaining milk and pour over cooled cake.

Cover with saran and chill until set.

Pour cherry pie filling over all.

Top with whipped cream and slivered almonds.

An easy version of the Black Forest Cake.
Who does not love the combination of cherries and chocolate!

Canteloupe with Wine Blueberry Sauce

1/2 c. white sugar
1 tbsp. cornstarch
3 thin slices lemon
3/4 c. port wine
2 c. blueberries
firm vanilla ice cream
peeled canteloupe rings

Combine sugar, cornstarch, lemon slices and port in a small saucepan.

Simmer for about 5 minutes or until clear.

Remove lemon slices, add blueberries and chill thoroughly.

Spoon ice cream into canteloupe rings and top with chilled blueberry mixture.

Serves 6-8.

This elegant dessert is featured on our cover.
Left-over sauce may be kept in a covered jar in the refrigerator.

Cherry Cheesecake

Graham Wafer Crust
1 1/4 c. graham wafer crumbs
1/4 c. melted butter

2 large bars cream cheese
2 tbsp. milk
1 c. icing sugar
2 pkgs. dessert topping
1 c. milk
2 tbsp. lemon juice
19 oz. tin cherry pie filling

Prepare crust and press into a 9" or 10" springform pan.
Bake at 375° for 7-8 minutes.

In large bowl, blend cheese with 2 tbsp. milk. Gradually add
icing sugar and beat on high speed until fluffy.

Combine dessert topping mix with 1 c. milk and prepare
according to package directions.

Add dessert topping and lemon juice to cheese mixture and beat
on high speed until well blended.

Pour over crust. Spoon pie filling over and refrigerate for 4
hours.

Variation: Omit lemon juice and fold 1 c. well-drained
crushed pineapple into batter. Top with graham crumbs
instead of pie filling.

Mincemeat Cheesecake

1 c. vanilla cookie crumbs
1/4 c. melted butter
1 3/4 c. mincemeat — add a little rum
4 c. miniature marshmallows
1/3 c. orange juice
2 large bars of cream cheese, softened
2 tsp. grated orange rind
1/2 pt. whipping cream, whipped

Combine crumbs and butter. Press in a 9" spring-form pan.

Bake at 325° for 10 minutes and cool.

Spread mincemeat on crust.

Melt marshmallows with orange juice and stir until smooth. Chill until thick.

Combine softened cheese and orange rind. Beat until well blended. Whip in the marshmallow mixture.

Fold in whipped cream and pour over mincemeat.

Chill until firm. Garnish with candied fruit.

A nice, light Christmas dessert.
Not as filling as mincemeat pie.

Donna's Chocolate Crème-De-Menthe Dessert

1 pkg. Peak Frean Bourbon Cremes (200 grams)
1/3 c. melted butter

1 small pkg. chocolate instant pudding
1 pkg. dream whip
1 1/4 c. milk
1/4 c. crème-de-menthe

Crush cremes and add melted butter.

Press into a 9" square pan and bake at 300° for 10 minutes.

Beat chocolate pudding, dream whip, milk and crème-de-menthe together until thick, about 5 minutes.

Pour on top of crust.

Sprinkle top with toasted, slivered almonds.

Chill well.

Variation: 1 1/4 c. chocolate wafer crumbs may be substituted
for the Bourbon Cremes.

Benjamin's Chocolate Mousse Cake

1 lb. white or dark chocolate of very high quality
— We used bitter-sweet
1/2 lb. unsalted butter
1 pt. whipping cream
2 whole eggs
4 egg yolks
4 egg whites

Crust
1 1/2 c. graham cracker crumbs
3 tbsp. unsalted butter melted (2 1/2 oz.)

Combine crumbs with melted butter and mix well.

Line 9" or 10" ungreased spring form pan with the mixture to a depth of 1/4" - 1/2".

Melt chocolate and butter in double boiler stirring until liquified.

Cool chocolate, butter mixture to room temperature and add 2 whole eggs and 4 egg yolks. Mix well.

In separate bowl, beat 4 egg whites until stiff.

Beat whipping cream until it is the same consistency of chocolate mixture at room temperature.

Slowly fold one-half the whipped cream and one-half the egg whites into chocolate butter.

Once blended, fold in remaining cream and egg whites until blended. Do not over-mix.

Pour onto crust, spread evenly and refrigerate 2 hours.

Double Chocolate Mousse Cake

7 oz. semi-sweet chocolate
1/4 lb. unsalted butter
7 eggs separated
1 c. white sugar
1 tsp. vanilla
1/8 tsp. cream of tartar

In saucepan melt chocolate and butter over low heat.

In large bowl beat egg yolks and 3/4 c. sugar until fluffy. (about 5 minutes).

Gradually beat in chocolate mixture and vanilla.

In another large bowl, beat egg whites with cream of tartar until peaks form, then gradually add remaining 1/4 c. sugar. Beat until stiff.

Carefully fold egg whites into chocolate mixture.

Pour 3/4 of the batter into a 9" springform pan. Cover and refrigerate remaining batter.

Bake cake at 325° for 35 minutes.

When cool, remove ring from pan. (Cake will drop).

Stir remaining batter and spread on top of cake and refrigerate until firm.

Frost top and sides with whipped cream frosting.

continued. . .

Double Chocolate Mousse Cake (continued)

Whipped Cream Frosting
Beat 1/2 pt. (1 c.) whipping cream until soft peaks form.

Add 1/3 c. sugar and 1 tsp. vanilla and beat until stiff.

Spread on cake and garnish with shaved chocolate if desired.

Refrigerate overnight.

May be frozen: Freeze uncovered until solid. Then wrap well and return to freezer.

May look complicated, but do try this.
It is an easy to prepare make-ahead for chocoholics!

Chocolate Sin Cake

4 tbsp. raisins
4 tbsp. brandy
7 oz. bitter-sweet chocolate
3 tbsp. water
1/2 c. butter softened
3 eggs separated
2/3 c. white sugar
1/2 c. ground pecans
4 1/2 tbsp. cake flour
1/4 tsp. salt
1/4 tsp. cream of tartar

Soak raisins in brandy for 1 hour.

Grease a 9" round cake pan, line with wax paper and grease and flour wax paper.

Melt chocolate and water and stir until smooth.

Stir in softened butter a little at a time and cool.

Beat egg yolks and sugar until thick and fold in chocolate mixture.

Combine nuts and flour and stir into batter.

Stir in raisins and brandy.

Beat egg whites until stiff and fold in chocolate mixture.

Pour into prepared pan and bake at 375° for 20-25 minutes until firm to touch.

Cool completely, then glaze.

continued. . .

Sin Cake (continued)

Glaze:
4 oz. bitter-sweet chocolate
4 tbsp. butter

Melt chocolate and butter together in double boiler over hot water.

Cool and pour over cake.

This is especially nice served with a thin custard and puréed raspberries mixed with a little sugar and brandy.

A chocolate lover's dream! Chocolate makes you _"crazy"_! We're all crazy over this one!

Gâteau Maison

graham wafers
1 pkg. vanilla pudding (the kind you cook)
1/2 pt. whipping cream, whipped
icing sugar and milk
chocolate sauce

Line an 8" × 8" pan with graham wafers.

Cook pudding according to directions and cool slightly, then pour over wafers.

Spread the whipped cream over pudding and add another layer of graham wafers.

Mix together enough icing sugar and milk to be thick enough to spread over top of wafers.

Dip a knife in the chocolate sauce and make a design over top.

Keep refrigerated.

This "House Cake" is easy but elegant.
Get the kids to make this one!

Gracie's Lemon Dessert

1 1/2 c. crushed graham wafers
1/4 c. white sugar
1/3 c. melted butter

Mix together and pack in a 13" × 9" baking pan, saving 1/4 c. for the top.

1 large tin carnation milk, chilled well
1 lemon — rind and juice
1 small lemon jello
3/4 c. hot water
1/2 c. white sugar

Beating carnation milk until very stiff, adding lemon rind and juice while beating. Milk must be *very* cold in order to whip.

Add sugar and beat well.

Dissolve jello in water, cool until mixture begins to set and add to the creamed mixture.

Pour over base and chill well.

Top with remaining crumbs.

Variation: Substitute 2 c. chocolate cookie crumbs for the graham wafers and omit the sugar for the crust. Substitute 1 pkg. lime jello for lemon in the filling.

An old, old favourite! Cool and refreshing!

May Levick's Meringue Torte

Set oven at 450°.

Grease bottom of a spring form pan.

6 egg whites
1/2 tsp. cream of tartar
1/4 tsp. salt
1 1/2 c. fine granulated sugar
1 tsp. vanilla
1/4 c. white rum
1/2 pt. whipping cream

Place egg whites in a large mixing bowl. (Make sure the bowl is free of grease and the eggs are at room temp.). Add cream of tartar and salt.

Beat egg whites slowly at first until the egg whites become foamy. Start adding the sugar a little at a time. The meringue will be stiff and shiny when done.

Scoop meringue into prepared pan. Put pan on middle shelf of oven. Turn OVEN OFF and leave overnight.

Release sides of pan. Make holes with skewer in the meringue and pour in rum. Cover with whipped cream and garnish with fruit. A big hit!

May, who taught Gourmet Cooking, was kind enough to share this marvelous dessert with us. It was certainly a gourmet ending to her gourmet meal!

Chocolate Mousse

1/2 pt. whipping cream
8 oz. pkg. semi-sweet chocolate
5 eggs, separated
Rum to taste — 2 tbsp. approx.

Scald cream.

Put chocolate and cream in a blender.

Add egg yolks and rum. Blend until smooth.

Beat egg whites until stiff but not dry.

Fold whites into chocolate mixture and chill overnight.

Mildred's Maple Mousse

6 egg yolks
3/4 c. maple syrup
1/8 tsp. salt

Cook egg yolks, maple syrup and salt in a double boiler and stir until thick.

When the mixture coats a spoon, remove and pour into a bowl. Beat until cold.

Whip one pt. whipping cream and fold lightly into custard.

Add 1/2 c. crush peanut brittle and place in a glass dish. Sprinkle more peanut brittle on top and freeze.

Remove from freezer 1/2 hour before serving.

Sex In A Pan

First Layer
1 c. finely chopped pecans
1 c. flour
1/2 c. butter or margarine, melted

Mix above ingredients together and press in a 9" × 13" pan.
Bake at 300° for 25 minutes. Cool.

Second Layer
1 large bar cream cheese (room temperature)
1 c. icing sugar
1 large tub (1 litre) Cool Whip

Whip cream cheese, icing sugar and 1/2 tub of Cool Whip
together and spread on top of first layer.

Third Layer
3 c. milk
1 pkg. instant chocolate pudding (4 serving size)
1 pkg. instant vanilla pudding (4 serving size)

Beat above ingredients together until thick and pour over cheese layer.

Top with remaining Cool Whip and sprinkle with two crushed
Crispy Crunch chocolate bars.

Sinfully good!
Like sex, a grande finale!

51

Sherry Trifle

1 16 oz. sponge cake or pound cake
2 1/2 c. custard or vanilla pudding
1/3 c. sherry or brandy
1 c. whipping cream
raspberry jam
slivered almonds

Cut cake in pieces and line a medium size glass bowl.

Spread cake with jam and sprinkle with sherry.

Make custard (we used Bird's custard powder), and pour over cake while warm.

Chill thoroughly.

Whip cream and spread over custard.

Decorate with toasted almonds.

Make ahead and refrigerate.

A splash of spirits makes the dessert!
An excellent trifle. May also be decorated with any fresh fruit.

Tin Roof Dessert

1 c. butter
1/2 c. brown sugar
2 c. flour
1 c. chopped pecans
1/2 gallon vanilla ice cream, softened
chocolate sauce

In a large roasting pan, cut butter into chunks. Add brown sugar, flour and pecans. Bake 400° for 20 minutes. Stir often for fear of burning.

Cool and set aside 1 1/2 c. of mixture.

Press remaining mixture into bottom of 9" × 13" pan.

Spread ice cream over and top with reserved crumb mixture.

Cover with foil and freeze 24 hours.

Chocolate Sauce
To 2 c. chocolate sauce, add 1 tbsp. chocolate liqueur.

Cut dessert in serving pieces and top with chocolate sauce.

Let stand 5-10 minutes before serving.

Doris' Walnut Torte Cake

9 large eggs (separated)
3/4 c. white sugar
5 tbsp sifted all purpose flour
1 tsp. baking powder
2 tbsp. bread crumbs
pinch of salt
1 c. ground walnuts

Break eggs and separate them into two large bowls. Beat egg yolks and sugar until double in size (about 10 minutes).

Sift together flour, baking powder and salt. Add walnuts and bread crumbs.

With clean, cold beaters, beat egg whites until very stiff.

Slowly fold above ingredients into beaten egg whites.

Pour batter evenly into 3 - 8" or 9" layer cake pans which have been lined with slightly greased wax paper. Bake 350° for 20-25 minutes. (Test with tooth pick) Cake should be a light gold colour.

Frosting
1 c. homogenized milk
3 tbsp. all purpose flour

Bring to a boil stirring constantly until thick. Cover and let cool completely.

Combine 1 tsp. instant coffee to 1 tsp. boiling water. Let cool.

continued. . .

Frosting (continued)
Beat 1/2 lb. <u>unsalted</u> butter with 1/3 c. white sugar with low speed until creamy, about 10 minutes.

Combine all frosting ingredients, beating at medium speed until very creamy.

Spread frosting between layers, on sides and on top of cake. Sprinkle top of cake with finely chopped walnuts for decoration.

The frosting on cake is a better texture when cake is kept cool.

This cake freezes well and sometimes tastes better after a few days. Cooled cake can be made ahead and frozen until ready to ice and serve.

This is an easy torte to prepare. Definitely Company fare, and our thanks to our neighbour Doris for sharing it with us.

Wilma's Chocolate Coconut Ice-Cream Dessert

1 large pkg. semi-sweet chocolate pieces (16 oz.)
1 large can evaporated milk
1 10 1/2 oz. pkg. miniature marshmallows
1 1/2 c. flaked coconut
6 tbsp. butter
2 c. rice krispies, crushed
1 c. chopped nuts
1/2 gal. vanilla ice-cream

In saucepan, melt chocolate and milk. Bring to a boil and boil gently for 4 minutes or until thick, stirring constantly.

Add marshmallows.

Beat and stir until melted. Chill.

In skillet, melt butter and stir in coconut. When brown, stir in nuts and cereal.

Spread 3 cups of cereal mixture in a 9" × 13" pan.

Soften ice-cream slightly and put 1/2 on top of crumbs.

Spread 1/2 chocolate mixture on top of ice cream.

Repeat the layers and top with remaining crumbs. Cover and freeze.

Cut in serving pieces and let stand at room temperature for 5-10 minutes before serving.

Serves 16

Topping for Angel Cake (1)

1 small pkg. pistachio instant pudding
1 c. cold milk
1 small carton cool whip

Blend milk and pudding until thick.

Fold in cool whip and spread on cake.

Refrigerate.

When strawberries are in season, use a strawberry instant pudding, or

when peaches are in season, use a peach instant pudding, etc.

Topping for Angel Cake (2)

2/3 c. sugar
2 tbsp. flour
2 eggs slightly beaten
1 c. crushed pineapple (1 small tin) undrained
3 tbsp. lemon juice
1/3 c. orange juice
1 c. whipping cream

Cook sugar, flour, eggs with pineapple until thick, stirring constantly.

Add juices. Cool.

When cool, fold in 1 c. cream, whipped.

Keep in refrigerator and use as needed, it's super!

Cookies
and
Bars

Chocolate Chip Oatmeal Cookies

3/4 c. flour
1/2 tsp. baking soda
1/2 tsp. salt
1/2 c. shortening or lard
1/3 c. white sugar
1/3 c. brown sugar
1/2 tsp. vanilla
1/4 tsp. water
1 egg
1 c. rolled oats
1 - 6 oz. pkg. chocolate chips

Blend shortening, sugars, vanilla and water.

Beat in egg.

Mix flour, baking soda and salt together and add to creamed mixture. Stir well.

Stir in oats and chocolate chips.

Drop on greased cookie sheet and bake at 375° for 10-12 minutes.

Butterscotch chips may be substituted for chocolate, if desired.

A favourite with your Cookie Monsters!

Extra Good Cookies

3/4 c. butter or margarine, softened
1 c. brown sugar
1 egg
2 good c. flour
1 tsp. ginger
1 tsp. cream of tartar
1 tsp. baking soda

Cream butter and sugar until fluffy.

Add egg and beat well.

Mix together flour, ginger, cream of tartar and baking soda and add to creamed mixture.

Stir until mixture forms a ball and chill.

When ready to bake, roll out dough and use your cookie cutters to make shapes.

Sprinkle with sugar and bake on a greased cookie sheet at 350° for about 10 minutes.

This old family favourite dates bake to 1921. Our kids loved to decorate these with coloured sugar at Christmas.

Ginger Snaps

1/2 c. butter or margarine
1/2 c. white sugar
1/4 c. brown sugar
1 egg
1 tbsp. molasses
1 1/3 c. flour
1 tsp. cream of tartar
1/2 tsp. baking soda
1/4 tsp. salt
1 tsp. ginger
1/4 tsp. cinnamon

Cream butter and sugars, mixing well.

Add egg and molasses and beat.

Mix flour, cream of tartar, baking soda, salt, ginger and cinnamon together and stir into creamed mixture. Mix well.

Chill dough.

Form into small balls and roll in mixture of:
   1/4 c. white sugar
   1/4 tsp. ginger
   1/2 tsp. cinnamon

Place on a greased cookie sheet, flatten with a fork dipped in cold water and bake in middle rack of oven at 350° for 10-15 minutes.

If you like ginger, try these! They are a "snap" to make!

Grandma's Jumbo Ginger Cookies

1/2 c. soft butter or margarine
1 c. white sugar
1 egg
1 tbsp. molasses
2 c. flour
1/2 tsp. baking soda
1/2 tsp. salt
1 tsp. ginger
1/2 tsp. nutmeg
1/4 tsp. cloves
3/4 c. buttermilk or sour milk
1 tsp. vanilla

Combine butter, sugar, egg and molasses and beat until smooth and fluffy.

Stir together flour, baking soda, salt and spices and add to creamed mixture alternately with sour milk and vanilla. Chill.

Drop by rounded tablespoons on greased cookie sheet and bake at 400° for 10-13 minutes, until lightly browned and top springs back when touched.

Spread with butter icing while slightly warm. Makes 2 dozen large cookies.

Butter Icing
1/4 c. soft butter
2 c. icing sugar
1 tsp. vanilla
2 tbsp. cream (approximately)

Combine, using enough cream to make thick icing that is easy to spread.

These are a soft cookie and a favourite of
Grandma Prange's grandchildren.

Peanut Butter Cookies

1/2 c. butter or margarine
1/2 c. peanut butter — We use chunky peanut butter
1/2 c. white sugar
1/2 c. brown sugar
1 egg
1 1/2 c. flour
1 tsp. baking soda
1/4 tsp. salt
1 tsp. vanilla

Cream butter, peanut butter and sugars until fluffy.

Add egg and beat well.

Mix flour, baking soda and salt together and stir into creamed mixture.

Add vanilla and stir.

Drop from teaspoon onto greased cookie sheet and press down with a fork that has been dipped in cold water.

Bake on middle rack of oven at 350° for 10-15 minutes.

Sister Joye used to say, "Add an egg and beet?"

Peanut Cookies

1/2 c. butter or margarine
1/2 c. brown sugar
1 egg
1/4 tsp. baking soda
1 tsp. baking powder
1 c. flour
1 tsp. vanilla
1/2 c. white sugar
1/2 c. oatmeal
1/2 c. cornflakes
1/2 lb. peanuts with skins

Cream butter and brown sugar. Add egg and beat well.

Combine flour, baking soda, baking powder and add gradually to creamed mixture, mixing well.

Stir in vanilla, white sugar, oatmeal, cornflakes and peanuts. Mix well.

Drop by small spoonfuls on greased cookie sheet. Top with a peanut if desired.

Bake at 375° for 8-10 minutes.

This wonderful crunchy, nutty cookie has been in our files for years.

Oatmeal Cookies

1 c. butter or margarine
1/2 c. white sugar
1/2 c. brown sugar
1 egg
1 tsp. vanilla
1 1/2 c. flour
1 1/2 c. oatmeal
1 c. coconut — optional
1 tsp. baking soda
1 tsp. salt

Cream butter and sugars until fluffy.

Add egg and beat well. Add vanilla.

Mix together flour, baking soda and salt and add to creamed mixture.

Stir in oatmeal and coconut.

Drop from teaspoon onto greased cookie sheet.

Bake on middle rack of oven at 350° for 12-15 minutes.

Everybody's favourite!
Your cookie jar should always be full of these!

Breezy Brownies

1 c. white sugar
1/2 c. butter or margarine
4 eggs
1/8 tsp. salt
1 10 oz. can of chocolate syrup
1 c. plus 1 tbsp. all purpose flour
1 c. chopped pecans.

Cream together butter and sugar.

Add eggs and salt.

Blend in chocolate syrup and nuts and pour into greased 9" × 13" pan.

Bake at 350° — 20 minutes.

Icing
1 1/2 c. white sugar
6 tbsp. butter or margarine
6 tbsp. milk (1/3 c.)
1/2 c. semi-sweet chocolate chips
1/2 c. pecans (optional)

Mix together sugar, butter and milk in a saucepan. Bring to a boil, cook and stir for 1 minute.

Add chocolate chips and beat well until all are melted. Add pecans and spread on warm brownies.

Cool and cut in bars. Freezes well.

Delicious and a "breeze" to make!

Butter Tart Squares

1 pkg. butterscotch chips
1/2 c. margarine or butter
1/2 c. brown sugar
1 1/2 c. flour
1 tsp. baking powder
1/2 tsp. salt

Melt chips and butter. Remove from heat and stir.

Mix dry ingredients together and stir into hot mixture.

Pack into greased 13" × 9" × 2" pan and bake at 350° for 15 minutes.

2 eggs
2 c. brown sugar
1 tsp. vanilla
1 tbsp. corn syrup
1 c. raisins
1/2 c. pecans or coconut
pinch salt
1 tbsp. melted butter

Beat all above ingredients together and pour over crust.

Bake at 350° for 25 minutes.

When cool cut into squares.

Gooey like a butter tart, but much easier to make!

Chipits Chocolate Toffee Bars

1 c. flour
1/4 c. sugar
1 c. butter, softened
3/4 c. firmly packed brown sugar
1 1/4 c. chopped nuts
1 c. chocolate chips and 1/2 c. peanut butter, melted together

Combine flour and sugar.

Cut in 1/2 c. butter and mix until mixture resembles coarse crumbs.

Press into ungreased 9" × 13" × 2" pan and bake at 350° for 15 minutes.

Mix brown sugar and remaining 1/2 c. of butter in a saucepan. Bring to boil, stirring constantly. Boil for 1 minute.

Pour evenly over the baked layer.

Sprinkle with nuts and bake for 15 minutes.

Remove from oven and ice with the chocolate peanut-butter mixture.

Cool and cut into squares.

Instant energy — just like a candy bar!

Date or Raisin Squares

1 3/4 c. rolled oats
1 c. packed brown sugar
1 1/2 c. flour
1 tsp. baking soda
1/4 tsp. salt
3/4 c. butter or margarine

<table>
<tr><td>

Date Filling
1 lb. dates
1/4 c. sugar
1 c. water
1 tbsp. lemon juice

</td><td>

Raisin Filling
3/4 c. brown sugar
3 tbsp. corn starch
1 1/4 c. water
1 1/2 - 2 c. of raisins
juice and grated rind of 1 lemon
1/2 c. chopped nuts

</td></tr>
</table>

In a bowl combine oats, sugar, flour, baking soda and salt. Cut in butter and mix until crumbly.

Press 1/2 of this mixture in greased 8" × 10" baking pan.

Cook ingredients for the filling of your choice until thick and smooth.

Spread filling over crumb mixture and sprinkle remaining crumb mixture over top.

Bake at 300° for 45 minutes or until lightly browned.

Cool and cut into squares.

Lemon Bars

1 c. plus 2 tbsp. flour
1/2 c. butter or margarine
1/4 c. powdered sugar
2 eggs, slightly beaten
1 c. white sugar
1/4 tsp. salt
3 tbsp. lemon juice
1/2 tsp. baking powder

Cream together 1 c. flour, butter and powdered sugar and press into a greased 8" square pan.

Bake at 350° for 20 minutes. Cool.

Mix together eggs, white sugar, salt and lemon juice.

Add remaining flour and baking powder. Mix well and pour over cooled crust.

Bake at 350° for 25 minutes.

Sprinkle top with powdered sugar as soon as removed from the oven.

Cool thoroughly and cut into bars.

Makes 16-24 bars.

Meta's Squares

20 graham wafers, crushed
1 heaping tbsp. flour
1/2 c. white sugar
1/2 c. melted butter

1 can condensed milk
2 c. coconut
cherries and nuts (optional)

Mix graham wafer crumbs, flour, sugar and melted butter and pack in an 8" × 8" square pan.

Bake at 325° for 15 minutes.

Mix the condensed milk, coconut, cherries and nuts and pour on top of crust.

Bake 15-20 minutes more.

Ice with a butter icing using a little cherry juice for colour.

Over the years, these squares have been served at many an afternoon tea party. Meta is known for her love of entertaining!

Peanut Butter Squares

1/2 c. brown sugar
1/2 c. corn syrup
1 c. peanut butter
2 c. corn flakes
1 c. rice krispies
1 tsp. vanilla

Heat brown sugar and corn syrup, just until sugar melts. Cool.

Mix the peanut butter, cereals and vanilla together and add to sugar and syrup mixture.

Pack in a greased 8" × 8" square pan and refrigerate. Ice and cut in bars.

Icing
1/2 c. brown sugar
3 tbsp. milk
1 tbsp. butter
1/2 tsp. vanilla

Mix above ingredients in a saucepan and bring to a boil. Boil 1 minute stirring constantly.

Cool and beat in 1 c. icing sugar.

Guaranteed to satisfy your sweet tooth!
(Assuming you still have one.)

Julia's Pumpkin Pie Squares

1 c. all purpose flour
1/2 c. packed brown sugar
1/2 c. oatmeal
1/2 c. butter

Combine the above ingredients and mix until crumbly.

Press mixture into a 13" × 9" greased pan and bake at 350° for 15 minutes.

Combine: 1 14 oz. can pumpkin
      1 large can of evaporated milk
      2 eggs
      3/4 c. white sugar
      1/2 tsp. salt
      1 tsp. cinnamon
      1/2 tsp. ginger
      1/4 tsp. nutmeg
      1/4 tsp. ground cloves

Pour mixture onto crumb crust and bake at 350° for 20 minutes.

In a small bowl combine: 1/2 c. chopped pecans
      1/2 c. packed brown sugar
      2 tbsp. butter

Sprinkle the above over pumpkin filling and return to oven.

Bake 15-20 minutes until set.

Cool and cut into squares.

Easier than a pumpkin pie and just as good!

Sweet Marie Bars

2 c. rice krispies
1 tbsp. butter melted
1/2 c. peanuts

Mix above ingredients together in a bowl.

Melt but do not boil: 1/2 c. brown sugar
⠀⠀⠀⠀⠀⠀⠀⠀⠀⠀⠀⠀⠀1/2 c. corn syrup
⠀⠀⠀⠀⠀⠀⠀⠀⠀⠀⠀⠀⠀1/2 c. peanut butter

Add to first mixture and mix well.

Press into greased 8" × 8" pan and chill.

Topping
1 - 6 oz. pkg. chocolate chips.
1 tbsp. butter

Melt chocolate chips and butter together until smooth and spread over chilled bars.

Cool, cut into squares and refrigerate.

Better than an "Oh Henry!"

Christmas
Goodies

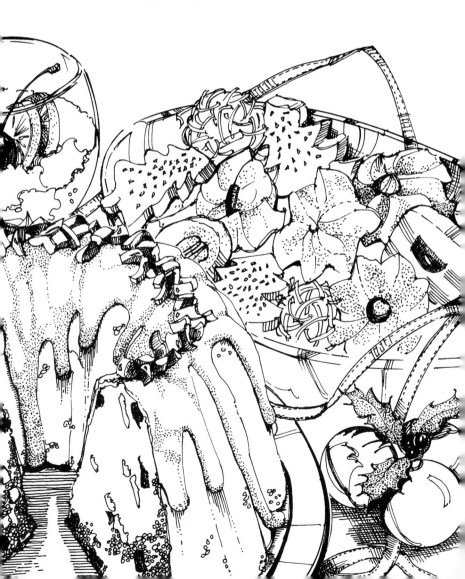

Almond Mice

1 c. softened butter
3 tsp. icing sugar
2 c. flour
1 c. ground unblanched almonds

Cream butter and icing sugar.

Add flour and mix well.

Add ground almonds and mix.

(May be refrigerated and baked later).

Form into little fingers and place on a cookie sheet.

Bake at 300° for 10 to 15 minutes.

While still warm, roll fingers in fruit sugar.

Store in covered tin in a cool place, away from cats and kids!

Nutmeg Butterballs

1 c. soft butter
1/2 c. sugar
1 tsp. vanilla
2 c. flour
1/8 tsp. salt
1 1/2 c. blanched, ground almonds
red candied cherries, halved

1/2 c. fruit sugar
2 tsp. nutmeg

Cream butter and sugar.

Add vanilla.

Mix dry ingredients together and add to creamed mixture. Chill.

Roll in balls and press a cherry half in the middle. Fold dough around cherry and place balls on a cookie sheet.

Bake at 300° for 15 minutes.

Roll in mixture of fruit sugar and nutmeg while warm.

Deck your plate with balls of nutmeg,
fa la la la la, la la la la!

Meringue Snow Caps

2 egg whites
1/2 tsp. peppermint extract
1/8 tsp. cream of tartar
dash salt
3/4 c. sugar
1 c. chocolate chips

Beat egg whites, peppermint extract, cream of tartar and salt until peaks form.

Gradually add the sugar and beat until stiff.

Fold in chocolate chips carefully.

Line cookie sheets with brown paper and drop by teaspoon on paper.

Bake at 325° for 20-25 minutes.

Turn oven off and leave cookies in oven to dry out for 1-2 hours.

Peanut Butter Dainties

1 c. peanut butter
1 c. corn syrup
1 c. brown sugar
2 c. cornflakes
2 c. rice krispies

Mix all above ingredients together, roll in balls and roll balls in coconut.

Keep refrigerated in covered cookie tin.

Pat's Pecan Crunch Cookies

1 c. butter
1/2 c. sugar
1 tsp. vanilla
1/2 c. crushed potato chips
1/2 c. chopped pecans
2 c. all purpose flour

Cream together butter, sugar and vanilla.

Add crushed potato chips and pecans.

Stir in flour.

Form into small balls, using about 1 tbsp. of dough each.

Place on ungreased cookie sheet.

Press balls flat.

If desired, sprinkle with red or green sugar, or top each cookie with a pecan or candied cherry.

Bake at 350° for 16-18 minutes or until cookies are lightly browned.

This recipe yields about 3 1/2 dozen cookies.
Ideal for your cookie exchange!

Mother's Shortbread

1 c. butter, softened
1 c. lard, softened
1 c. brown sugar
4 c. flour

Cream butter and lard together.

Mix in brown sugar and cream well.

Add flour, 1 cup at a time, mixing well after each addition.

Mix well with hands, adding more flour until dough doesn't stick to your hands.

Form into large ball and refrigerate.

Cut dough into pieces and pat with hands — or roll on floured board to 1/4" thickness.

Cut into shapes with cookie cutters and bake at 300° for 20 minutes or until light brown.

The very best shortbread ever! All Mother's friends will agree! Hopefully we can carry on her tradition of making that extra batch to share with others.

Pigs In A Blanket
or
Date and Cheese Rolls

1 small bar (250 grams) Velveeta cheese, softened
6 tbsp. butter or shortening
1/2 tsp. salt
2 c. flour
2 tsp. baking powder

Cream the cheese and butter or shortening together.

Add dry ingredients, mixing well. Use hands to work in the flour.

Chill for three hours, or overnight.

Roll dough thin and cut into small circles.

Place a piece of date on circle and roll up, pressing the edges of dough together.

Place on cookie sheet and bake at 400° until brown — about 5 minutes. They won't take long to bake.

Roll in fine white sugar while still warm.

Don't "hog" these, serve them!

Swedish Tea Rings

1/4 c. brown sugar
1/2 c. butter, softened
1 c. flour
1 egg, separated

Cream butter and sugar.

Add slightly beaten egg yolk.

Add the flour and mix well.

Form into small balls and dip in slightly beaten egg white, then in crushed nuts or coconut.

Make a dent in the centre of each cookie with the back of a spoon and bake at 350° for 5 minutes.

Make the dent deeper and bake for 15 minutes more.

When serving, fill the centres of the the cookies with red jelly.

These are a colourful addition to your Christmas cookie plate.

Walnut Crescents

1 c. soft butter
1/4 c. icing sugar
2 tsp. vanilla
1 3/4 c. flour
1 c. chopped walnuts
icing sugar

Cream butter and sugar well. Add vanilla.

Stir in flour and mix well. Add walnuts.

Chill the dough until easy to handle.

Using a teaspoon of dough per crescent, place on cookie sheet and bake at 350° for 10 minutes.

Cool slightly and roll in icing sugar.

Rich, like shortbread. At Christmastime your
cookies should be extra special like these.

Festive Fruit Ring

1 c. butter, softened
1 pkg. (250 grams) cream cheese, softened
1 1/2 c. white sugar
1 tsp. vanilla
2 tsp. grated lemon or orange rind (optional)
4 eggs
1 3/4 c. all purpose flour
1 1/2 tsp. baking powder
1/2 c. seedless raisins
1/2 c. golden raisins
1/2 c. mixed fruit
1/2 c. candied red cherries
1/2 c. chopped nuts
1/4 c. all purpose flour

Cream butter and cream cheese with electric mixer. Add sugar and cream well.

Beat in vanilla and lemon rind.

Add eggs, one at a time, beating after each addition.

Mix flour and baking powder and blend in.

Combine fruit and nuts and 1/4 c. flour and stir into batter.

Pour into greased and floured bundt or tube pan and bake at 300° for 70-80 minutes or until done.

Cool 10 minutes. Remove from pan and cool completely.

Either dust cake with icing sugar, or mix icing sugar and milk together until of pouring consistency and drizzle glaze over top.

Auntie Lib's Christmas Cake

1 lb. red candied cherries, quartered
   (save about 15 whole ones for top).
1/2 lb. green candied cherries, quartered
3 lbs. seedless raisins
2 lbs. light raisins
1/2 lb. mixed peel
1/2 lb. mixed candied fruit
1/2 lb. blanched almonds, ground,
   saving 15 whole blanched almo~ ` for top of cake
1 lb. butter
2 c. brown sugar
4 c. flour
10 eggs, separated
1 tsp. baking soda mixed with 1 tbsp. of sour cream
1 wine glass of sherry or orange juice
1 tsp. cinnamon
1 tsp ginger
1 tsp. nutmeg

Wash and dry raisins. Add peel and all the fruit.

Cream butter and sugar.

Add beaten egg yolks a little at a time.

Add soda and sour cream mixture.

Sprinkle 2 c. flour over fruit and mix well.

Mix 2 c. flour with spices and add to the creamed mixture
alternately with sherry or orange juice.

Beat egg whites until stiff and add alternately with fruit and nuts.

continued . . .

Auntie Lib's Christmas Cake (continued)

Grease 1 set of 3 Christmas cake tins, line with brown paper and grease again.

Fill tins half full with batter.

Press whole red cherries in the corners and in the middle of the batter.

Fill tins with remaining batter.

Press whole cherries and whole almonds into batter.

Place a pan of water in the oven.

Bake in a 250° oven for 3 - 3 1/2 hours.

Small cake will be done in 3 hours.

While cakes are still warm, pour a little sherry or brandy over top.

Cool cakes for 2 hours before removing from tins, and wrap in foil.

*Although this is another of our Christmas traditions,
Mother used this recipe for her four daughters' Wedding Cakes.*

Grandma Prange's Christmas Pudding

1 1/4 c. flour
1 tsp. baking soda
1 tsp. cinnamon
1/2 tsp. nutmeg
1/2 tsp. salt
1 c. brown sugar
1/2 c. chopped suet
1 c. grated carrot
1 c. grated potato
1/4 c. rum, or milk

1/4 c. flour
1/2 c. raisins
1/4 c. mixed peel
1/3 c. glazed pineapple

In a large bowl, mix the first group of ingredients, mixing well after each addition.

In a small bowl, mix second group of ingredients and add to first mixture.

Grease a 2 qt. round cake tin.

Pour in batter and decorate top with red and green glazed cherries.

Cover top of pan with waxed paper and tie down.

Put water in a large pot and place cake pan on rack into pot.

Cover and steam for 3 1/2 hours at a gentle boil, adding water if necessary.

continued . . .

Grandma Prange's Christmas Pudding (continued)

<u>Rum Sauce</u>
1 c. brown sugar
1 c. whipping cream
1 tbsp. rum

Place sugar and cream in saucepan and boil gently, until thickened.

Remove from heat and add rum. Serve hot!

(Pudding may be re-heated in a steamer or microwave oven.)

Ruth's Christmas Eggnog

1 bottle L.C.B.O. alcohol
12 large egg yolks
1 lb. icing sugar
1 pkg. vanilla sugar (Oetker)
16 oz. tin carnation milk

Mix egg yolks and sugars on slow speed.

Add carnation milk and alcohol, mixing well.

Bottle and store in a cool place. Improves with age!

What is Christmas without a little nog?
Be sure to serve only a <u>little</u>, or you'll "nog off"
like our friend Fanny and miss dinner!

Metric Equivalent Chart
For The Kitchen

Rounded

1 tablespoon (tbsp.) . . . . 15 ml

1 teaspoon (tsp.) . . . . 5 ml

1/2 teaspoon . . . . 2 ml

1/4 teaspoon . . . . 1 ml

1/4 cup (c.) . . . . 50 ml

1/3 cup . . . . 75 ml

1/2 cup . . . . 125 ml

2/3 cup . . . . 150 ml

3/4 cup . . . . 175 ml

1 cup . . . . 225 ml

A Great Idea For:

Showers, bridge prizes, stocking stuffers, host or hostess gift, or just an inexpensive gift for sweet lovers.

Please send me:

_____ copies of Muffin Mania
at $6.95 per copy

_____ copies of La Manie des Muffins
at $6.95 per copy

_____ copies of Nibble Mania
at $6.95 per copy

_____ copies of Veggie Mania
at $6.95 per copy

_____ copies of Sweet Mania
at $6.95 per copy

Plus $1.00 per copy for mailing.

Enclosed is $ _____

Name _____

Street _____

City _____

Province _____ Postal Code _____

Make cheque payable to:

Muffin Mania Publishing Co.,
c/o Mrs. Cathy Prange,
184 Lydia St.,
Kitchener, Ont
N2H 1W1

Notes

Notes

Notes

Notes

Notes